SCHOLASTIC
News
Nonfiction Readers

Sunny Weather Days

by Pam Rosenberg

Children's Press®
A Division of Scholastic Inc.
New York Toronto London Auckland Sydney
Mexico City New Delhi Hong Kong
Danbury, Connecticut

These content vocabulary word builders are for grades 1–2.
Subject Consultants: Robert Van Winkle, Chief Meteorologist, WBBH, Fort Myers, Florida; and Jack Williams, Public Outreach Coordinator, American Meteorological Society, Boston, Massachusetts

Reading Consultant: Cecilia Minden-Cupp, PhD, Former Director of the Language and Literacy Program, Harvard Graduate School of Education, Cambridge, Massachusetts

Photographs © 2007: age fotostock/Raymond Forbes: 23 top right; Alamy Images: 1, 23 top left (Enigma), back cover, 7 (Photo Network); Corbis Images: 5 bottom left, 16 (Bohemian Nomad Picturemakers), 5 top left, 14 (Mark Bolton), 19 top left (Tony Demin), 5 bottom right, 6 (Michael Keller), 19 bottom right (Roy Morsch), 20 left (Richard Ransier), 4 bottom left, 9, 13, 17, 20 right, 21 center, 21 top (Royalty-Free), 4 top, 8 (Jed and Kaoru Share), 19 top right (Ariel Skelly), 19 bottom left (Tom Stewart), 5 top right, 10 (Steve Terrill), 21 bottom (Third Eye Images); Dembinsky Photo Assoc./Dan Dempster: 2, 15; Getty Images: cover (Ryan McVay/Taxi), 23 bottom right, 23 bottom left (SW Productions/Photodisc Green); Photo Researchers, NY/Detlev Van Ravenswaay: 4 bottom right, 12; Superstock, Inc./Tom Rosenthal: 11.

Book Design: Simonsays Design!
Book Production: The Design Lab

Library of Congress Cataloging-in-Publication Data

Rosenberg, Pam.
  Sunny weather days / Pam Rosenberg.
    p. cm. — (Scholastic news nonfiction readers)
  Includes index.
  ISBN-10: 0-531-16770-4
  ISBN-13: 978-0-531-16770-0
  1. Sunshine—Juvenile literature. I. Title. II. Series.
  QC911.2.T78 2007
  551.5'271—dc22   2006013307

1 2 3 4 5 6 7 8 9 10 R 16 15 14 13 12 11 10 09 08 07

CONTENTS

WORD HUNT

Look for these words as you read. They will be in **bold**.

buds
(buhdz)

sprinkler
(**springk**-lur)

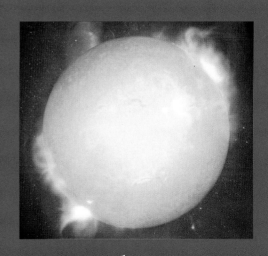

star
(star)

4

plants
(plants)

pumpkins
(**puhmp**-kinz)

sunburn
(**suhn**-burn)

sunscreen
(**suhn**-skreen)

A Sunny Day

Get your sunglasses and **sunscreen**. It's going to be a sunny day. Let's go outside and have some fun!

sunscreen

Sunglasses help protect your eyes on a sunny day.

The warm spring sun helps trees and flowers grow. You can see the flower **buds** and new green leaves.

Sunny summer days can be hot. Playing in water can help you keep cool.

buds

Playing in the water from a sprinkler is a good way to stay cool on a hot, sunny day.

Sunny fall days are cool and crisp. They are perfect for picking apples and **pumpkins**.

On winter days the sun may shine but the air can be very cold. Bundle up before going outside to play!

pumpkins

Sunny winter days are perfect for sledding.

What is the Sun? The Sun is a **star**. A star is a ball of hot, glowing gas. The Sun is the closest star to Earth. That is why we feel its heat and see its bright light.

star

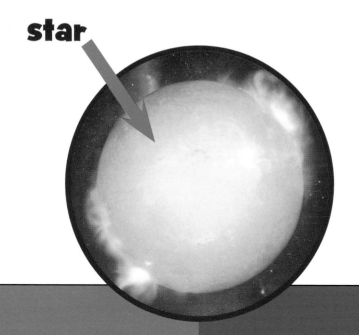

You can't see the sun on cloudy days.
But it is still shining behind the clouds.

People and animals need the Sun's light and heat to stay alive.

Plants need sunshine to grow. Their green leaves capture the Sun's energy. They use the Sun's energy to make food.

plants

A butterfly's body needs to be warm so it can fly.

People need the Sun's light and heat, too. The warm sunlight makes playing outside possible.

But the Sun's light rays are strong. They can burn your skin if you are not careful. Then you get a **sunburn**.

sunburn

Play in the shade. It can help you protect your skin from sunburn on a sunny day.

It is fun to be outside on sunny days. You can bike, swim, or play sports. What is your favorite thing to do on a sunny weather day?

SHADOW HUNT

A shadow is a dark shape made when something blocks the light from the sun. Can you tell what made these shadows?

(ANSWERS: 1. boy, 2. dog, 3. tree, 4. bird, 5. airplane)

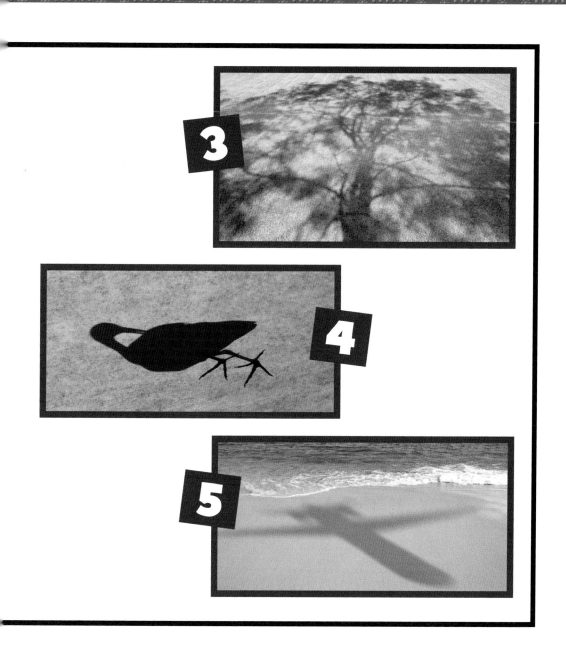

YOUR NEW WORDS

buds (buhdz) parts of plants that will grow into leaves or flowers

plants (plants) a living thing that uses sunlight and water to make food

pumpkins (**puhmp**-kinz) round, orange fruit that grows on vines on the ground

sprinkler (**springk**-lur) a tool that attaches to a hose and sprays water

star (star) a ball of burning gases in space

sunburn (**suhn**-burn) sore, red skin that you get from staying in the sunlight too long

sunscreen (**suhn**-skreen) a cream or lotion that is put on skin to protect it from the sun's harmful rays

BE SMART ABOUT PLAYING IN THE SUN

Wear a hat and sunglasses.

Wear sunscreen.

Drink lots of water.

Spend some time in the shade.

INDEX

animals, 14
apples, 10

biking, 18
buds, 8

fall, 10
flowers, 8

leaves, 8, 14

people, 14, 16
plants, 14
pumpkins, 10

sports, 18
stars, 12
summer, 8
Sun, 12, 14, 16
sunburn, 16
sunglasses, 6

sunscreen, 6
swimming, 18

trees, 8

water, 8
winter, 10

FIND OUT MORE
Book:
Goldstein, Margaret J. *The Sun.* Minneapolis, MN: Lerner Publications, 2003.

Web site:
National Weather Service for Kids
http://www.weather.gov/om/reachout/kidspage.shtml

MEET THE AUTHOR:
Pam Rosenberg is an editor and author of children's books. She lives in Arlington Heights, Illinois. She likes to spend sunny weather days with her kids, Sarah and Jake, and her husband, Peter.